STILL STANDING
BY GRACE

The Journey
Only You Stop You

by

TRACY BYARS

Unless otherwise indicated, all Scripture quotations are taken from the King James Version.

Copyright © 2018 by Tracy Byars. All rights Reserved.

ISBN-13: 978-0-692-12817-6

BUILD A HOUSE PUBLISHING

All Accent added to scripture quotations is the author's.

Printed in the United State of America 2018

Dedication

This book is dedicated to the Almighty God who has given me life and the Grace to walk through the process of my purpose on this earth, so that I may have eternity with him once it's all said and done. I also want to honor my late mother, Wanda Hart for birthing me. I was able to watch her spiritual /faithful life line of loyalty and serving generously as the peaceful woman she was.

The consistent love that she would show to the people she loved by her actions while she was on earth, until the day she crossed over to be with the Lord. Mama your love was amazing (selfless).

One of my mother's favorite songs was "Amazing Grace", The song says, "Amazing Grace, how sweet the sound, that saved a wretch like me. I once was lost, but now am found, was blind but now I see."

Acknowledgements

I just want to thank God for the strength and grace He has bestowed upon me to bring this timing work to a completion.

I also want to thank my beloved children, my daughter, Kawanna Byars - Williams (My First Born), my sons Brian Daniels Jr. and Darius Williams Sr. Also, my other daughter (my miracle baby) Bri'an Daniels. And my six beautiful grand babies, you guys really kept me smiling and my head above water.

To my beloved mid-wives, Mengesha Keelen (Best Friend), Prophetess Erica Dees Pace, Pastor Joycelyn Ruffin, and Larry Byars (my brother) that encouraged me through my testing and process. They held up my arms in prayer non-stop. Thank you so much for your unfailing love through my roller coaster ride. I've gained so much strength from you all being by my side and not leaving me.

To Mission Church, the group of praying sisters' (Ruth) and the other ladies that accepted me in with so much love. And Pastor Scott, thank you for the timing and wise counsel that restocked my spirit with wisdom (words) that I will never forget!

To the beautiful Prophet ET Odonkor (Matilda Odonkor), thank you for your faithful friendship of support and prayers through my journey and keeping your word.

Thank you Prophet Glendon (Tina Jones) for that prophecy in North Carolina that shook the foundation of my life, my, my, and everything played through just as spoken.

Introduction

The Grace of God is when you can't even wrap your mind around His goodness or explain how you have made it through those tough seasons; especially when you take the time to reflect over your life and all you've been through. God spared your life and enabled you to keep unspeakable, unexplainable joy, and love in your heart. He granted you the Grace to be in your right mind! Yes, it was God that enabled you to endure the waves of life without the residue of unforgiveness, bitterness, hatred or retaliation.

I dedicate this book to anyone that is in a dark place because of your wrong choices or maybe even your right choices. It is the Holy Spirit that gives you the genuine Grace of understanding; to walk through your process with God by endurance, long suffering, and patience because, "Only You Stop You". As you continue to Stand because God Graced you to, I pray that every trial that you experience is designed only for your making and shaping, and that you understand that through the testing period, there's an expiration date and cut off time. When all is finished, I pray that you'll lift your head and realize that it was His "Amazing Grace" that has kept you safe.

Foreword

Lady Tracy Byars has been a close friend to my family and I for some years now. We have shared moments in prayer together in the middle of the night when all seemed to be dark and gloomy and great testimonies of God's goodness when light appeared at the end of the tunnel.

While you flip through the pages of this book, one thing I can confidently say about my friend, Tracy, is that she is an intelligent, relentless woman of God with unfeigned faith who also believes in the virtue of hard work.

All these attributes are reflected in the time and detail spent on this timely piece, which will be a blessing to you, your family, ministry and business at large.

Her story is authentic and spells out the availability of God's grace for sustenance and preservation to all men in the face of life's storms, which we can always tap into – an attestation to her personal mantra, "Only You Stop You".

May you draw strength for your journey and inspiration for all your aspirations as you read this book and embrace the truth that God's grace is always available for you no matter the circumstance.

- **Prophet ET Odonkor**

(Global Commission - President)

Endorsement

Evangelist Tracy Byars is not only a true, anointed woman of God; an entrepreneur and a soon-to-be author; but she is a great friend indeed. Tracy and I have shared a close bond of friendship for over 9+ years. She is the epitome of a virtuous woman and the love she has in her heart spews over unselfishly into every life she encounters.

This masterpiece that she has written reveals her inner strength, tenacity, courage and the grace that she possesses that was birthed out of pain, struggles and trials. But the good news is that pain was not her ending, but a spiritual incubator that produced purpose and this thought provoking read.

This book brings to life a story that was supposed to have come to an end a long time ago but the conclusion of the matter is "Victory". It is an insightful guide to assist you in different areas of life. As you read, may your heart be filled with hope that allows your faith to say, "I can do all things through Christ which strengthens me!". And as you glean from her powerful testimony, may it catapult you from the ditches of life into your Divine destiny! Now get up and live! And in the words of my dear sister, "Only You Stop You!"

- Pastor Joycelyn M. Ruffin

Chapter Contents

Chapter 1: The Beginning 14
Jeremiah 1:5

Chapter 2: Teen Troubles 20
Philippians 1:6

Chapter 3: The First Time..................................31
Amos 3:3

Chapter 4: I Surrendered..................................39

Chapter 5: The Transformation 62
Romans 12:2

Chapter 6: A New Start with Bishop 87
Mark 10:8

Chapter 7: The Final Storm............................118
Ephesians 6:12

Chapter 8: New Mantel, New Wings................133
Through The Eyes of Bri

Chapter 1

I was the sixth child of 8 children brought up in a household of hardworking business owners, my mother and stepfather. At a very early age, I was put to work without compliant. As a child, I was very bold, happy, and outgoing. I was also a very curious child that loved outside and meeting people. My neighbors and I were in everybody's house from sun-up to sun-down. From my youth, I've always loved God. Many of my neighbors told me about Jesus, and I would find myself listening to bible stories they would tell me or read to me. There were also times I would even find myself attending church with them, when invited.

I was particularly close to one of my siblings, Larry Byars; he was 1 year my senior. When I wasn't working with my dad at the service station or our restaurant, Larry and I would find ourselves knocking on neighborhood doors looking for ways to earn money. We would politely ask our neighbors if they needed anything from the corner store, and we would shop for them to earn money. Larry and I did everything together; we both would walk to the nearby Catholic Church and anoint our heads with holy water and pray. However, I always felt responsible for my brother because he was born with Muscular Dystrophy. When we were younger, his life was normal, but the older he got, his muscles weakened, so he was prone to getting hurt more when we were playing outside.

I've witnessed so many miraculous healings concerning my family as a child. Larry stayed in and out of Children's Hospital. Surgery after surgery (eye surgery, back surgery), I witnessed the doctors tell my mother that my brother would be in a wheel chair soon and that he would not live to see 12 years of age. Also, if he ever wanted to drive, he would need to have equipment in his vehicle. My brother Larry is now 45 years old, still walking, no wheelchair, and no equipment in his vehicle! This is a miracle!

School was a challenge for me, I loved school and had perfect attendance all my life; I never missed a day of school. All of my teachers loved me, they all would call me their baby. My first-grade teacher liked me so much. I would bring her a honeybun and Pepsi every day, and she would keep me back a year to repeat her class. As I became much older, the school began to detect that I was struggling in the areas of speech and learning (comprehension). There were times my teacher would pull me out of my regular classes, and I would hate it. As a child, I asked myself why I was separated from my peers but didn't have the intellectual knowledge to answer that question. So, during that time, it caused me to rebel as a way of dealing with my insecurities. I had become an angry child and a class clown and began to display mean behavior towards my teachers, talking back and acting up; it was non-stop. I was so stubborn and played around so much in school that I was failing in every subject. It was like there were two sides of me as a child; the good Tracy began to wrestle with the bad Tracy. There was a part of me that wanted help and another part that didn't. However, my mom had no clue what was going on with me.

It's crazy how my mom never disciplined us as children; she was never stern enough to stick to punishment. I still got things like new clothes, money, and gifts, so my attitude was, "Oh well, I didn't have to show any effort in anything. I'm still going to get whatever I want." As a child, I didn't have a story of ever doing without, but our house had other dark stories that went on for years. Those hidden secrets begin to unfold when I became a teenager. I watched my mom go through so much manipulation by the enemy and compromising with my step-father. She sacrificed this so that her children could have a better life. Watching the cycles of what my mother allowed was not a good thing for me to see, because it caused a molding and shaping in my life. I believed the wrong things that people do were acceptable, and setting boundaries was never necessary. My mother was such a strong woman, but she just didn't have the strength to leave and the faith to know that she could make it on her own without a man. So, she did what many other women do, ignore truth and compromise for keeps.

Chapter 2

The next chapter of my life, I was off to middle school. It was a very exciting time for me. I loved school, but I struggled; my focus on keeping up with my friends was "real." I never remembered receiving help with my homework as a child after school. My parents were great financial providers but lacked concern or didn't help when it came to school homework because they were always busy working.

I started working at the age of seven years old. By the age of twelve, my dad would leave me alone to run the restaurant that was next to our service station. My step dad taught me how to operate the register, take orders, count the money, cook, prepare orders, and much more. When pay day came around, my step father would have us to put 1/4 of our earnings into our bank account for Christmas savings. As a child, I was taught the importance of paying bills on time, good credit, and money management. However, in school I was failing in my behavioral reports, reading, spelling, and English. Coping with struggling in school and becoming a teenager was confusing. So, my only way of expressing the lack of communication was to rebel even more as a teen.

The rebellious spirit I had opened the doors to so many other spirits in my life. I chose all the wrong friends who were close to me because of what I had lots of money in middle school. People knew it because they would always see me stopping at the corner store before school, buying lots of junk food. I've always loved people, had a big heart for my friends, and loved giving. Having money was like a magnet because of my constant giving. I didn't know that at the time.

There was this girl I met named Mary; I liked her because she was cool.. Mary would leave school to smoke cigarettes. It was like she would come to school in the morning, but during lunch when the bell would ring, she would leave school campus. Mary had this "don't care" attitude. One day, she asked me, "Do you want to leave school, and come with me home?" , "How can we both leave school without the teachers seeing us walk out the gate?" I countered. She responded, "Watch me." and I followed her. At that very moment, my whole childhood changed for the worse. It doesn't take much for a child that was already struggling in school to lose interest in school. When I think back, what amazes me to this day is none of the middle school teachers noticed we were gone. Getting away with that became a cycle of cutting school. When Mary and I would walk to her house, she would smoke cigarettes, after cigarettes; she let me try one, but I choked and that was the last cigarette I ever smoked.

When we would arrive to Mary's house, her mom would be laying on the bed sleeping with cigarettes and beer cans all around. Her mom would not say anything to her; she would let Mary do whatever she wanted to do. I really thought that was cool. Mary also introduced me to this performing arts school she attended. We talked to the guy that was the head of the singing and dancing teachers at this location. He asked me what type of talents I had and to sing for him. Now you know I was excited because, as a little girl, I was very bold and loved singing and dancing for people. The performance teacher heard me sing and was like, "Wow I like her!" So, I asked my mom if I could join the school, and my mom said yes. Every day after school, Mary and I would go to practice, which was awesome. We would dress up in costumes and do performances on stage of all the hit songs that were popular back then. Michael Jackson's "I Want You Back," Whitney Houston's "How would I Know," and many other hit songs.

There was this boy that attended the school, and Mary wanted me to meet him! Mary was said he's cute and that his name was Denis.

When I first met him, I said out loud, "Ugh, he's ugly." Denis then held his head down and walked out the door. I was mean to boys at that time because I did not have much interest in them. However, a change of heart came over me when I saw him perform on stage for the very first time. He sang my favorite song, "I want you back," by Michael Jackson! I loved Michael Jackson back then, so I started liking Denis. It was humorous looking back on it. Denis and I would see each other every day after school. He attended another middle school, but we would always see each other at performing school. There were times my mom would pick me up, or I would catch the bus home. I would love catching the bus home after practice because that gave me more time to be with Denis. My first real boyfriend! We would hold hands, and he would always walk me to the bus stop to catch the bus home. He was my first love. There was nothing but smiles and more disobedience because of my choices. Denis and his brothers would cut school too, just like Mary did. For so long, I really couldn't discern the devil's devices in my life.

I was surrounded by a group of friends that focused more on fun and not education. So, I began to lose interest for school more and more each and every day, just to be with him. Mary's mama didn't care, Denis's mama didn't either, but my mom did. I was playing like I was going to school each day, but I didn't. It went on for months, then the middle school I was attending at the time noticed my weeks of absences and called my mom. Boy was I scared when my mom pulled up and spotted me sitting outside with Denis and his brothers. She told me to get in the car. It was like I was scared but had a rebellious spirit of not caring. As time went on, I finally made it out of Middle School.

In High School, I noticed a change in my body and I didn't know what was going on. No menstrual cycle but still clueless. I hid being pregnant wearing a girdle my 9th grade year for 6 months! I would wear big shirts and hold my stomach in when being approached by teachers and friends. My mother didn't notice until one day she asked me did my period come and I said, "No." She took me to the doctor and he said "Yes, your daughter is 6 months pregnant." My mom was crushed but didn't shed a tear; she was numb. I went through mixed emotions and said, "I don't want it." I wanted to abort it or have it and give it up for adoption. During this time, I lost all likings for Denis and hid out during my whole pregnancy from him. I was already behind in school, and I felt so embarrassed. (It's something how I'm sitting here writing this. I'm reminiscing over somethings that I've put in the back of my mind.) My heart is heavy because I can feel my mom's pain. My mom always supported me in the things I wanted to do and always spoke highly about me to people. Now my mom was disappointed in me. To think back on the harm I could have caused to my unborn child by wearing those tight girdles throughout my pregnancy...wow! Jesus will always grace us in the midst of our ignorance.

15 years old, having a beautiful baby girl 6lbs 10 oz., it was a long delivery. After my mom began to sort things out, she contacted Denis's parents about the baby's birth; they paid for a nursery for her. A little while later, I went back to school, but I felt as if I didn't belong there. I continued to go to school, fighting every feeling of shame, and another problem surfaced. Denis's parents started missing payments for the nursery. I was pulled out of school because I had to tend to my own child and my mother was working. After I turned 16, as a high school dropout, I was doing what mothers do, getting her dressed, catching the bus, and taking her to doctor appointments.

Real life hit me so fast, I really did not have the freedom to be a child. I had to woman up!

My mom and I would rotate with watching my daughter, so in the evening while my mom wasn't working, I would be working. Things began to fall apart with my daughter and her father because he was still immature. However, his parents would always try to push him to take on his responsibilities. When he didn't, they would always step up to the plate with helping me take care of our child.

Chapter 3

The struggle of not having the freedom as a child was real. By the time I was turning 18 years old, my baby was turning 3 years-old. One day, I decided to go to a club with a good friend of mine. I used to love to dance, so it was nothing for me to take the floor. I met this guy named Brian. We danced all night, laughed, and had great conversation. As the night ended, he asked me for my phone number, and I left the party with my friend. A couple of days passed by, and I receive a call from Brian and he asking for "Tamika" (wrong name). Right then and there, I should have shut him down, but I didn't. I was so naïve. I just corrected him.

Now, this boy, Brian, was handsome! He had beautiful brown eyes and was fit; I had really fallen for him. Brian didn't have a car, so he would send for me and my daughter by cab. He would be waiting outside once we got to the destination and pay the cab driver. Since I was 18 at the time, I was like wow; I loved that feeling. Brian would always have money and buy me whatever I wanted. He was always concerned about my needs. Brian had a very laid back and quiet spirit; all the girls liked him. He played football as a running back in Highschool. Boy, did Brian have the charm. Now Brian and I are in a serious relationship. He told me that he had a child, and the baby was a few months old. But this happened before our relationship. He and the child's mother grew apart because they used to fight a lot. As time went on, the journey with Brian was up and down. I was living all over the place, by his sister's house in the projects, my friend's house, and sometimes back home with my mother. There were times, when I was causing problems at home with my mother, so he would come pick me up and pay for me a hotel room, so we both could spend time together. However, nothing could stop Brian from being Brian. He was always running the streets. I was that young girl full of self-faith, thinking I could help a man change. I really got myself tangled up with a young man that was fatherless all his life, that had no discipline, that sold drugs, messed with a lot of women, made babies, and was stamped by the state as a career criminal with cycles of misdemeanor charges all his life. Brian grew up in a household of 12 siblings, no father. He was raised by his grandmother, but his mother was present , and he was the baby boy of the family. He never had discipline in his life, he was always open to doing whatever he wanted to do.

My life took a big shift. You know the saying "good girls like bad boys"? Well that was my journey. While I was with Brian, my mother kept my daughter; she said she didn't want her grandchild being all over the place. For a child my age, those were the words I wanted to hear. I would run back to Brian, who lived with his sister in the Lafitte Project, and stay with Brian around the area where he sold drugs. They called that area "The SET." I went with him in drug houses, watched him cook up coke and turn it into rocks; I was also there to help him cut it up and bag it. There were also times I would hold the drugs in my bra. All of this wasn't Brian's choice for me. He didn't want me around him while he was doing those things, but I insisted and thought I could keep him from getting in trouble. The Grace of God was truly hovering over the ignorance of my mind. Brian would give me his drug money to hold for him and send me home to my mother. He felt that made me more secure in our relationship. As time went on, I got pregnant by Brian, and during the time of my pregnancy, I went to the doctor for a checkup, and the doctor told me that I had like 3 different types of sexually transmitted diseases caused by my partner having sex with different woman. One of the diseases would cause our son to be born blind. After I left the doctor's office, I informed Brian and looked over the danger of my body then begin to share my medications with him. I was prescribed to take 6 pills a day until everything was cleared up. I was so in love with Brian that I was unconcerned about my own health. As time went on, I started to plan to move out of my mother's house. I worked and saved money to rent my first home. I got a job at a Supermarket in the deli department until a week before my due date. I finally rented my first home. Brian, myself, and our son were living together. To my surprise, it didn't keep Brian coming home every night as I thought it would. Brian was still running the street and coming home whenever he wanted to. Brian was a great provider but didn't know how to be a family man. As years passed on, it was an ongoing journey of Brian selling drugs and being in and out of jail. That left me always on my own and being the one to bail him out of his mess every time. I was a loyal woman, never set boundaries, and forever compromised every time he went to jail. I was always the one to pick up the pieces; work has been ingrained in me since I was a child, so a job was nothing for me to find. Brian and I finally got married at the court house; I remember that day like it was yesterday. It was pouring down raining and I was thinking, "My, my, my…does this mean my marriage and the endurance of it will be a storm?" I stayed in and out of court with Brian; he got off so many cases they had evidence on, God was so gracious over Brian's life. I really thought in my mind that he needed me; I couldn't leave him, and one day he would change. When the scripture says God looks beyond our faults and sees our needs, it is a true statement. I was young, disobedient, immature, and ignorant but would always find time to pray and God would always show me grace. Yes, God is more concerned with our becoming through our molding process. Grace on top of grace, nobody but God!

Chapter 4

A few months after all of the court hearings, I found out I was pregnant again by Brian.

My son was currently 5, and I was excited because I wanted a daughter from him. I was still going through all the same changes with him. My body was so stressed out, I remember being on the phone with one of my good friends. I was about 5 months pregnant at the time, and I felt a hard pain that went across my stomach. When I mentioned it to my friend, she was like, "Girl that's probably gas," so I thought nothing of it. The next week, I went for my routine checkup and my doctors looked at me shocked and told me to go straight to the hospital to get an ultrasound done. My doctor would not tell me what was going on and neither did the ultrasound lady. When I went back to see my doctor, he told me my baby was dead and he needed to give me a DNC. Tears begin to roll down my face and the doctor begin to speak words of encouragement to me. He said, "Tracy, sometimes these things happen. Maybe the development of the baby was not healthy." After I left the doctor's office, I called Brian and told him what happened. He was quiet on the phone, but still wasn't as concerned; he was still doing him. When it was time for me to be admitted to the hospital, for them to take the baby, Brian dropped me off then left. He was nowhere to be found.

There were many times that I felt extreme pain. Brian was causing me heartache. There were no other way to express my broken heart but through lashing out, wanting to fight him, and calling him out his name. One day, I was in prayer and asked the Lord to change Brian, and God said, "No, I want to start with you because two wrongs don't make anything right. Brian is a whore monger and what are you? I need to deliver you from your mouth." One late night, my 2 kids and I were on our way to pick up Brian from work. My kids were sleep in the car, did not have on seat belts, and were laid across the seat. When I got to a 4-way light (intersection), I was waiting at a red light and then my light turned green. As I began to cross, I heard sirens loud, coming towards me. However, I didn't know where it was coming from. The police car came crashing into us; the whole drivers side of the car was pushed to the passenger side. All I could hear was silence, then people's voices asking me was I okay and my two kids crying. We were rushed to the Hospital and was told that we were hit by a police car, driving over a 100mph. My forehead was swollen with glass in it and the doctors began to remove the glass, shaved my hair off my head, and stitched me up. Kawanna's (my daughter) eye was swollen shut and her spleens were divided (she was rushed to Children's Hospital). My son had a few bruises, but he was fine. We all could've been dead that night, but nothing but the Grace of God was over our life. Kawanna stayed in Children's Hospital for a whole week. Her swelling went down, her spleens came back together with no surgery at all, and she was discharged.

A couple of years went by, I realized that I couldn't do this alone. I really needed God. I got fed-up, tired of the cycles, and stopped running from God. I decided to give myself completely over to God. I begin to set boundaries in my house and told Brian I didn't want him to bring anything else stolen to my house. While he was running the streets, getting young girls pregnant, my kids and I were attending church, and God was strengthening me for the next chapter of my life. I began to feel myself outgrowing a lot of the foolishness I tolerated for years. I remember one night, I called the church prayer line and a mother from the church answered the phone. I briefly explained what I was going through, and she prayed for me. She asked

God to give my husband Brian a wakeup call but spare his life. That same night I got a call at about 12 A.M. saying that my husband Brian was in the emergency room. He was shot in the eye, but the bullet was still in his head. It replayed constantly; it was like God had already prepared me for it. I rushed over to the hospital and saw him lying there. They had other emergency surgeries that were critical, so they had Brian waiting in line for about 6 hours before they started surgery on him. After surgery, we found out he lost his eye, the bullet was still plugged against his skull, and that type of surgery would be deadly. During that time, my faith was on a high level; I was a baby in Christ and excited about the goodness of God. I would go to the hospital every day, pray over Brian, and sing "No Weapon Formed

Against Me Will Prosper." Brian made it out of the hospital, and I brought him home; he was on some heavy meds. While we were at home, I heard a hard knock on the door from the police asking for Brian. I asked them what they wanted because he just was discharged from the hospital after being shot in the eye. The policemen told me that Brian was being charged with child rape because he was dating a minor, and the young lady was pregnant. I was like, "What?" My heart almost fell from my chest, but I convinced the cops not to arrest him. I went into my prayer closet with God because I couldn't talk to Brian as he was on a high dosage of meds. Now, I'm praying and fussing with God, asking God, "How can you give this young girl a baby with my husband?" I lost my baby two years ago. As weeks went on, after the healing of Brian, as I was taking care of him, I found out that I was pregnant again. This young girl was about 16 weeks pregnant, and I was like 6 weeks pregnant! Now, I decided to fight for my marriage and compromise with it all. I felt it was something God would want me to do. I still attended church and found my peace with God and let Brian do whatever he wanted to do, and his behavior remained the same.

As time passed along, it was my 40th week going into my pregnancy. I got a call that Brian was arrested again, and his court date was scheduled for the following Monday. Brian was sentenced to 7 years in jail. My heart dropped, and his heart did too. It was the beginning of a brand-new chapter of my life. I didn't know at the time, but it was God protecting me from all the drama. He was sparing Brian's life as well. God knew I didn't have the strength to leave this unhealthy marriage, and I needed his help to really get ahead in moving into my purpose and what was already predestined for my life.

Brian was a great provider but didn't know how to be a husband or a father. During those 7 years, my whole life took a turn for the best! I continued to support Brian while he was incarcerated. I made sure money was on the phone so he could call, money was in his account, and the kids and I visited him. I was attending church faithfully and joined a prayer group. I began to see my whole perspective changed concerning my goals and dreams.

That was something Brian wasn't comfortable with because I wasn't as available as I used to be for him. I began planning for me and the kids' futures. First thing was cleaning up my credit and his (Brian) while he was in jail. I bought my first dream home, and God's blessings began to overshadow me all the more as I was in position. I joined a church, and the Pastor of the church licensed me to be the head Evangelist of the Evangelism Ministry. We would go out every Saturday of the month, walking the streets, inviting souls to the ministry, and feeding and clothing people. This went on for many years, and through that time, God blessed me with a job that I wasn't qualified for. The New Orleans Public School Board's was able to pay my Mortgage with one week's pay.

I still was planning to make sure everything was straight for Brian's return home. I had faith to believe that those 7 years would change him. As time got shorter for Brian, my life had become stronger. My spiritual life and relationship with God blossomed. I remember one night, I was praying and talking to God, and He asked me, "Was I ready for this?" (for Brian's return) and I said, "Yes." When the time came for me to pick Brian up on his release date, I was financially well off. Our life was set for us both without excuses. On my way home from picking him up, we stopped to buy him a new wardrobe because nothing he had could fit him anymore. Soon as we got home, our baby girl, Bri, saw her dad, looked at him, and asked, "Ma, can we bring him back?" Not knowing at the time, she saw something I failed to see. I replied back to her and laughed, "We didn't buy him from the store, so we can't return him."

As time went on, Brian got a job he wasn't qualified for. The people loved him at the job. He explained to them his past (time in jail), but they overrode his felony and still decided to permanently hire him after six months of him proving his work ethics. Brian was a very likable, meek, hardworking and humble guy. However, the demons of his past continued to hunt him. I remember lying next to Brian when we were sleeping, and I would have Prophetic dreams concerning him going back to his past. The holy spirit would tell me to tell him that God would remove me if he went back to his past. Brian would look at me and laugh. I remember in one of the dreams, he was walking out the door with his bags.

One particular day, it felt kind of strange; Brian went to work and didn't return home that night. I got on my knees and began to pray; never have I asked God to give me the strength to accept his will for this marriage, but I did that night and felt the power of God saturate me. When I got up from off of my knees, I felt a change come over me. Brian came through the door several hours later, and I asked him to leave. I saw that he was trying to take me back to the past, but the Lord gave me instructions on the do's and the don'ts with him. No more manipulation and compromising! I shut down all points of contact with him in August of 2007, I filed for my divorce, and it was finalized by December of 2007. The last words Brian told me was, "Tracy, thank you for the life, my life will no longer be the same. You are a good woman and I don't know what is going to happen to me."

Through the marriage, I came to a place with God of acknowledging that my marriage was based on my choices from the very beginning. There's no way in life any person that rejects having an intimate relationship with God would ever walk in the light of making the right choices for his or her life. I've come to realize, over the years of growing through it all, that every marriage isn't called by God, some were put together due to the choices we have made through ignorance and through our life's journey. No person can ever force love on another, otherwise we will be placing our hearts in the wrong hands. But it is God's Grace that keeps us and covers us through our process. There are some people we tend to outgrow through the years because our prospective towards life becomes much clearer in pleasing God. When I look back and reflect on the 17 years I invested in my relationship with my children's father, I feel as if God was teaching me how to serve the most difficult man and delivered me from my mouth by teaching me self-control. God also taught me how to love and forgive when it was the hardest of the hardest. The Bible talks about how we need to love on people that are not always the most lovable. As God began to instruct me through the closure of the marriage, through all the purging, plucking, molding, and the necessary enhancements of my life that had strengthened me to become the Woman of God I am, God stripped the voice of the enemy off of me, the lies of manipulation (feeling I was responsible for Brian's soul), strengthened my heart, and prepared my hands for war by loving Brian enough to let him go and move forward with my own life for the sake of my children, my own sanity, and happiness. I made a vow to God that I would no longer compromise my soul for an unrighteousness type of living. I would stand for or even die for God's TRUTH and Principles.

Going into our 2nd year of my divorce from Brian, I was focused on working in ministry by witnessing, feeding the hungry, and liturgical dancing as well. Now God is really beginning to deal with me more in my dreams, prophetically. He was giving me dreams about myself and what is yet to come and dreams about others. There's were times I even experienced outer body visitations of me walking with God through hell and seeing people scream out for freedom. (The temperature in hell was so hot that the flesh was falling off of people and it was to a point where you couldn't even breath.) My relationship became even closer with God; I tapped into another realm that I never knew existed. God was dealing with me in strange ways in the spiritual realm while I was still dealing with the natural responsibilities in my home. I have always been a parent, never putting work or ministry before my kids. I've always gave them my time and instilled good morals in them. However, I do know that kids can come from the best homes/upbringing and still rebel. When my son turned 14 years old and just started high school, he started to act up in school by rebelling, staying out late, not coming home at night, and even, I found out, taking ecstasy pills with his friends. Everything was out of control with my son. The only thing I knew how to do was pray and turn over all things to God. I stayed focused by taking care of God's business and holding God at his word to take care of mines. I would leave the house and take a box of bibles with me and walk the streets of New Orleans, giving them out. It was also therapeutic to me, during this time, when the attacks against my children and my purpose were raging.

There were times my son would be out all night, come home, and want to sleep all day. When Sunday came around, I refused to compromise with the devil (As for Me and My House We Would Serve the Lord). I would make him get up and out of the bed and make him come to church in whatever he had on. We would get to church, and he would sleep the whole drive there, thinking he was going to just sleep in the truck while we were in church. I would put him out of my truck, lock the doors, and he would refuse to go inside. He would just sit outside the church, while we were in church. Now, I remind you, I was an active leader in church, over the Evangelism Ministry. I would be assisting the new members class (those that where new converts to the church). My son would be sitting outside for hours, until one day he got tired of sitting outside. He came inside and started sitting on the last pew in the back of the church.

One day, I was leaving Bible class and received a call from the Kenner police department saying that they arrested my son and two other boys for armed robbery. My son never went to jail for anything prior to this. I'm thinking from past experiences with his father that I can just get him a lawyer because this is his first time. I was over the top disappointed in my son but knew his disobedience was going to lead him into trouble. I even told my son the week before that there's some people that can get away with a lot and there's some people that one thing can cost them their entire life. Once I got down to the police station, my son was so green; he had already talked to the officers and told them what he did and that he had the gun. The other two boys knew not to talk because they had been to jail before. The officers taped my son and used that against him in court. I paid two different lawyers $5,000 apiece, and they both promised me that they would help my son, but they didn't.

The state took over my son's case and charged my son as an adult; they gave him (first offender)15 years in prison. I felt as if I couldn't breathe; I felt as if I was reliving his father's trial. Except this is my baby boy. The state took my son from me and placed him with adult murderers, rapist, and heavy offenders. I went home and sobbed like I never have in my whole life. This hurt was so different because it was my only son. My son had a future and plans to play football the next year in high school. It was his 10th grade year at Magnate High School, and he received a scholarship for college. I shut completely down because I couldn't grasp what was happening. I felt I was reliving with him what I just came out of with his father, and the prison he had to do his time at was the same prison his uncle and his dad did many years at. One of my biggest prayers was that my son would never follow the bloodline curses of his father and that his feet never would touch the jail cell. What happens when the very thing you prayed for not to happen wines up happening? That is really when you really begin to see what truly resides inside of you for Christ. It's something because every dark place I've ever been in, God never allowed me to stay in longer than I should've for some reason. He has always snatched me out for some reason. Fight just begin to rise in me, and I just begin to fight a little harder for my son. My son really had the strength and focus of his mother being in prison. In his first 3 months of him being in prison, he received his GED and started tutoring other inmates that were trying to achieve theirs. My son also received his lumber/welding certificate, discipleship, and about 10 other certificates within the first year of being in jail. God was causing things to work out for his good; God is faithful to His word.

Chapter 5

Three years went by since my divorce. I was extremely focused on ministry, and I was not open to any relationships.

I remember, one day, I was on social media posting, advertising my business, and I see a chat post pop up saying, "Hello, I just left your town." Normally, I block my chats and never chat with people I don't know, but I replied to him (The Bishop), "Oh, you were here doing ministry work?" He replied, "Call me." I left the page we were chatting on, googled him, and began researching who he was. He was getting inpatient and inboxed me again and said, "Call me." So, I inboxed him my number so that he could call me. When he called me, I was really quiet on the phone. I wanted to feel him out, and he really had a very exciting, happy spirit. However, he was just a little aggressive and doing a little bragging that was a bit unattractive, but I still decided to hear him out. Our conversation was good; he was talking about his life goals and all. I begin to stop him in the conversation and told him that I'm not a woman that's moved by all talk from a man, I'm a woman that's moved by actions only. He assured me that he didn't have time for games after all he has been through over the years. We talked for a while that day, and I was asking him a lot of questions. I had to pull back from talking to him to get clearance from God in who he was. He was calling me too much, and he was very aggressive. I overlooked it because I knew when a man was really interested a woman, he does the chasing. When I say, I loved this man's Spirit, his prayer life, and faith, I mean I loved it. Now at this point in my life, I'm not looking but waiting on God's man to be a part of my life, a true man of God.

The night before I went to bed, I asked God to show me who this Bishop was that was walking into my life. Prophetic dreams were one of the giftings I received from God as a child. This has always been the way God spoke to me and I would always ask the Holy Spirit to cover my dreams. When I had fallen asleep that evening, I had a dream of the Bishop and me running through the wilderness, he was protecting and fighting for me. When I woke up from the dream, I was shocked but didn't say anything to the Bishop when he called me the next day. We continued talking on the phone, I remind you he was doing all the talking, as I was still feeling him out. He said to me, "Tracy give me your heart, and I promise to take care of it". I was quiet, but he didn't know what was taking place on my end. I felt God right that minute. When I went to bed after I got off the phone with him, I had the same dream for the 2nd time. That was when I really knew it was God! It wasn't until then that I released all walls that was up concerning the Bishop. During that time, he was living in Atlanta, and I was living in Kenner, LA. We were both courting every day, we were face timing for hours and hours. During that time, he was living with a friend. Changes were still going on in his life, and he moved to a hotel room. I never thought anything of his transition because it didn't matter to me after what God showed me in a dream. That I was safe with him.

Now that I was safe, I was able to be open about my life. We were both going through transitions in our lives. Although, I owned my own home, I had a few bumps in the road financially due to my divorce. I had my own business. I was very active in ministry as a leader still. I served as head evangelist over the evangelistic ministry. I was secure and had accomplished much. I had been in a seventeen-year marriage to my children's father, which ended in divorce. I opened up to him about my son being in prison due to following the wrong crowd.

During the time of us courting, I received several phone calls, one from a friend he lived with prior to us meeting. His friend stated that he was not a licensed Bishop and he had conned many women by allowing them to believe he wanted to marry them. I also received a phone call from an unknown woman warning me to get away from him, that he was going to hurt me by breaking my heart the same way he broke her heart. She said the same words his friend had just spoken to me. He had been making promises to a lot of women, that he was going to marry them. I was in love, and I didn't hold him hostage to his past. I really didn't know these people, and I was holding on to what God showed me. I looked over it all, even though he had divorced

3 times before me. I was treated with love and respect during our courtship, and he never gave me any reason to doubt his love for me. I let my guards down, I was ready to love again. I was really excited to meet a true man of God and build ministry with him.

Eventually Bishop came to visit, and I introduced him to my mother and family. He stayed at my house but respected what I wanted and my holiness until marriage. He slept on my living room couch the whole time he was in town. When he flew back home, we continued face timing each other. We really enjoyed each other, and our relationship began to grow. He was always in good spirits and his mood was consistent regardless of what he was going through and that was so attractive to me. He didn't have a car, so he did most of his traveling on buses and trains. His living wasn't stable, but the way he handled the blows of life was more attractive to me than anything. We had so many similarities concerning life. When life throws you lemons, you make lemonade. I knew deep down in my spirit that we were going to be an unstoppable powerful team, and God was going to bless our lives together.

I genuinely cared for him with no strings attached, and I really believed he felt the same. We began to exchange our gifting expertise, and I cleared up his credit within the time frame of 3 months. At that time, he was good with graphic designing, so he started doing different flyers to enhance my business. We complemented each other, and I was at awe about the brightness of our future. I felt oneness between us. Things started to get better for him; he moved into his own apartment in the Atlanta area. As time went on, he started talking about marriage, stating he wanted to get married right away. I wanted to wait, and I explained to him why. I just wanted to experience a real wedding this time around. The Bishop was really an aggressive man and kept stressing marriage. We both decided to get married first, then have our ceremony afterwards. We began to plan everything, and everything was coming together. My plans were to sell my home and move to Atlanta, but The Bishop insisted that he relocate and come live with me. I really didn't like the idea because I was ready for change and wanted to experience something new. During that time, he was hosting Atlanta Live Broadcast, and he invited me and a close friend of mines to be guests on the show. While in Atlanta, we made the decision to apply for our marriage license and for him to relocate to Louisiana. During this time, we still weren't married, and we were living together. This didn't set right with us as leaders. We decided to get married shortly after and have a wedding ceremony later. Things were beautiful! We had so much fun together, we both were free-spirited people.

Happiness was in the air. I was on the path to a new life until one day I received a call from my ex-husband's brother saying my last two children's father was dead due to an overdose. He said they needed me and Bishop to take over his eulogy because the insurance policies his mother had for him were very small. My ex in-laws really loved me and trusted me. They knew all that I had been through with their brother for 17 years and that I was a good wife to him. So, the Bishop and I pulled everything together and were not paid one cent. My heart beat was never bitter towards my children's father. I had to lay my children's father to rest on the account of them. My ex in-laws were so grateful, accepting, and thanked my new husband (Bishop) for opening his heart to do something that many men would have never done.

All things were moving as planned. We had our wedding ceremony, planning to buy a bigger home, and building a ministry together. This was an exciting heartfelt dream a woman that loves the Lord really looks forward to with her Man of God. We found Bishop a good paying job through a temporary staffing agency that I knew personally. I remember one day he came home from work, and I began to see a change in him. He started to complain, and it went on and off the whole time while he was working. I tried to understand and encourage him, but it fell on deaf ears. Experiencing this behavior was all new to me. I was used to a man proudly providing for his family, so hearing a man complain about being a provider was a turn-off. But I kept my opinion to myself. We set goals; we met some and were on track to achieve many more. We were a great team; we had unmovable faith and a crazy zeal together.

One night we were sitting watching a movie, and he decided to get up. He wanted to go to bed, but I wasn't ready to go to sleep. I experienced him getting mad and going off, saying we were supposed to be going to bed together. I was so surprised at his behavior; it wasn't like this had always occurred with us not going to sleep together. I am the type of woman to keep the peace in her home. Often, I brushed things off and compromised with him.

The month of our wedding ceremony had arrived, and we were both excited. Everything was paid for and our boxes were packed because we were in the process of purchasing a new home as well. Three days before our wedding ceremony, we both were asleep, and he woke up to use the bath room. I heard a "boom," jumped up, and found him on the bathroom floor. I rushed him to the hospital (thank God, the hospital was 3 minutes from where we lived). They ran tests, said that his blood pressure was extremely high, and they were trying to find out why, so they could bring it down. They were running so many different tests on him and couldn't find out the problem. It was like a day before our wedding ceremony, and he told the nurses that he couldn't miss the wedding. He discharged himself at his own consent out of the hospital.

At this time, I look back and recall that Bishop's family wasn't in or at our wedding.

The only person that was there from his side was a longtime friend of his with his companion. One of his daughters also warned my oldest daughter when they were talking on the phone that I shouldn't marry her dad because he had been married too many times and had hurt women. I really didn't think anything of it. There were a lot of things I trusted the Bishop to handle and take control of. I really respected him as being my King (Boaz), the man of God I married. I felt safe in the midst of his flaws. I was willing to stand by and help him through it all because love covers all. The things that he possessed that I was attracted to were his love for God, prayer life, his unstoppable zeal, and his energized spirit. That overrode any other hidden thing that he probably had been dealing with. Through our relationship, we had the best of times together, like lovers and buddies. We did everything together; we were inseparable. I think I was more of the easy going one, wanting to keep peace, going along with everything he wanted or did because I trusted his intelligence and the man of God he was.

We had just started the ministry in New Orleans East. All of my family and friends supported us through the grand opening of the ministry and some even joined the ministry, but as time went on, they begin to tell me the negative things they were experiencing with him. His rudeness and his controlling ways. I am the type of person that will find peace in every situation, so I would take up for him and talk them into seeing a brighter side of things. I wouldn't tell him anything because I wanted to keep peace and didn't want to experience his defensive outburst that I had previously experienced.

I recall one exhausting day I had. I was extremely tired and rejected having sex with him for the very first time, and he just went off using scriptures trying to talk me into it, and not just that, he started calling his bishop friends trying to get them to talk to me. It was so unbelievable that night, I couldn't seem to wrap my mind around what was really going on. The Bishop was hollering, slamming doors, and all. I was thinking to myself, "What have I've got myself into." This was the beginning of the manipulation and the controlling spirit. The next day, I told him don't ever scream at me again because I'm not a child nor is he my sergeant, knowing that part of him came from the abuse of his time in the military.

Grace was given! We finally found our home that God wanted to bless us with. It was a 4-bedroom beautiful home in a beautiful new subdivision recently built for us in a small country town, and we were happy. Now we lived in Kenner, LA. We were packing, doing ministry, and still getting things situated till the closing on our new home. I remember as if it was yesterday. It was a Saturday night and church was the next day. That night, I was so exhausted from all of the nonstop work, so I went to bed early. I was in the bed sleeping, and he came in the room mad trying to wake me up for sex. I was so tired I told him, "Later bae, please I'm so tired." Now, I do want to clarify this, him and I would normally have sex every night consistently. But the minute I would say that I'm tired, which was not often, he would never have the consideration to respect my wants. That night I experienced him in a very frightening way. It was like something came over him, and he started screaming and hollering again slamming the doors threatening to leave me and fly back to Atlanta. Me not wanting to go back and forth with him, I just got back in the bed hoping he would calm down. He goes in the living room then came back in the bedroom and very aggressively rips all my clothes off saying, "Ok, you don't want to have sex with me, what's going on with you?" I was so scared and shocked that night, I didn't want anything to do with him at all. That Sunday morning when he woke up, he didn't say sorry or even try to settle anything. He just woke up like nothing happened and thought I was just going to go along with brushing his behavior off like I normally do. I didn't get dressed to go with him to church because I refused to sit in the house of the Lord being fake and comply with what I just experienced with him the night before. When he came home from church I was still quiet, and he begin to cry and explain to me that his day was the hardest day he ever had to face because everybody was asking where was First-lady, and he didn't know what to say, then he began to apologize for what happened.

One day I was sitting and thinking back on some of the things he shared with me in the very beginning of our courting about his past childhood traumas and began to realize that his past had molded him into the man he became. I begin to realize that he wasn't aware of his consistent behavior of outburst, of lack of self-control and not holding himself accountable for his actions and waking up the next day like nothing ever happened. As time went on, God was still blessing our union, things were happening quick for us. Moving day came around and we were all packed; one big truck relocated us to a new, quiet and country area 25 minutes from where we lived. We also started a church at the recreation center in the small town we were living in. We were just on fire for the Lord and focused on growing ministry. I was extra excited about all of what God was doing through us both. I was new at being a First Lady, but I had been in ministry for ten years. I was skilled in leadership. I was equipped for the position of First Lady, but I kept a strong prayer life and stayed educating myself for my position of the support he needed from me. The Bishop was the kind of a man that just made decisions on his own about the ministry. I had to adjust to his ways of making many decisions without me. As his wife, I should have been included in all decisions because I was his wife. He was a very private type of a person, which didn't bother me, but as time went on, it began to bother me. He was real guarded over his belongings and that was kind of strange to me, but I just let things be because I trusted him.

Bishop came in the relationship with several women friends. It really didn't bother me much at first; however, as time went on it, it became a problem for me. He would meet females while we were out, be it business or not, and exchange phone numbers. I was very uncomfortable with this because many of the women seek counseling after joining the ministry. He made the decision to counsel the lady members without the presence of the First Lady. This became a continuous issue for me knowing the protocol of ministry. I would express my concerns, but there were defensive outburst, and he did not consider my feelings. He stated, "God called me to be the head over the church and make decisions, not you." I began to shut down my feelings concerning the ministry with the attempt to stop arguing. My intentions were never to control the ministry; I only wanted us to work as a team, building

God's ministry and making sure boundaries were set in place so there was no room for the devil to invade God's assignment. I said to myself, "Lord what have I married? I'm an orderly woman that has balance. I tended to the needs of our home, kids, Ministry, my business and him with no lack, and also when I cooked, I brought his plates to him. I treat this man with the utmost respect and look how he treats me at times. As years went on, I begin to experience Bishop's interacting with many new people that had walked into our life later down the line; he's fussing with them over the phone, and they were no longer friends. I wasn't the only person experiencing his uncontrollable behavior. The heartbreaking thing was he never thought he was wrong or saw himself as the problem. I began to see the retaliation of his actions towards people that he was mad with; this had me crying on the inside.

Chapter 6

Our ministry journey began in New Orleans, Louisiana and ended in Hammond, Louisiana. We began working hard to build the ministry non-stop. We did evangelizing, fundraising, and lots of advertising to grow the ministry. We experienced many families and leaders join the ministry and leave the ministry. We had one family to join the ministry. I want to identify this family as the "treasure" family; their son was a musician, and they were seasoned leaders, their expertise was finances. They were a big part of the ministry and helped build the ministry while contributing financially, emotionally, and psychically. This family was truly a blessing. In the beginning of the relationship with this new family, I was very casual with them because I've experienced so many uncomfortable incidents with the Bishop becoming very close with previous members and turning them against me. As time went on, I started feeling vibes and seeing changes being made to the ministry without me being included. The Bishop would honor other people's opinions instead of his own wife's opinion. I was feeling so excluded but pulled more on God in prayer for strength to bear it without saying a word to avoid his outburst and lack of control. This family was there for us tremendously. When our car was in the shop having repairs done, they loaned us their extra car; when it was time for us to look for another church building, they did all the necessary work on the inside by building, and their whole family contributed their services for weeks and hours to make sure the church was completed. When we moved into our new business building, they helped us with the touch-ups. They were "really" God sent! I watched the Bishop become very close to Mrs. Treasure, and I'm sitting back knowing pretty soon, with his habitual behavior of getting close to people, it will soon fall apart because of the constant abuse of his month. I would notice Mrs. Treasure talking to Bishop everyday not just about church, but also about other things. Mrs. Treasure began to invite her family and other families to the ministry but made a big mistake in telling Bishop about their downfalls that would soon be taken advantage of by him. One of the families that she invited winded up joining the ministry.

Now, the wife of this family seemed to be a very nice young lady but had some serious issues that her husband had dealt with at a prior church with her. Not knowing this at the time, she seemed to be a nice young lady; she would complement me all the time about how beautiful I was, and she loved the way I dressed. Me being me, I opened up myself loving on God's people but knew we as leaders had to set boundaries for the respect of our position. The young lady and I became a little too close, and I begin to give her personal information about how I was still in great condition and ideas about my expertise in beauty enhancements. As time went on, the husband of this young lady became close to Bishop, and I believed all was going well with us and our members. I remember Bishop started to act really strange with. He would take a bath and afterwards leave the house late in the afternoon and say he's about to go to the store. Now, this particular night, my intuition led me to check his location on my iPhone, and I saw that he was parked at a park just sitting there but didn't think nothing of it and brushed it off. As time went on, I begin to experience more brush offs and dryness from him, but my intuition was telling me something is really going on with him because this was a new type of behavior. I hadn't dealt with this before. One day he asked me to drop him off at the new building because he wanted to go do some work there. As I'm about to leave the building, he texts me by mistaken saying, "She's leaving out the door now. You are welcome to call me now." When I get the text, he's shocked but switches things up quick and says I am making a big deal out of nothing; he was texting his best friend. A week had passed, and he wakes up one day and asks me to drop him off at the massage place. The whole time in the car, the spirit on him was not pleasant, so I'm just praying to myself quietly. I dropped him off and got back home; I went in his office, decided to go on his iPad, and see him conversing with the young married woman that's a member of our church. In the conversation, he was telling her that he was tired of me and that I don't want to see him happy and she replied back, "Babe don't worry about her enjoy your massage." He was thanking her for purchasing the massage for him. My heart completely drops as I'm reading these messages; I'm in a state of disbelief, so as I began to read previous messages, proof and truth are coming to the surface. They both are having an affair. This had been going on for about a month now, meeting at the park, the new church building, and having lunch together. This young lady's husband shared with me that this is not the first time he had to deal with his wife having an affair. She did this with the last Pastor. I took snap shots of as much of their conversations as I could for proof because I know the Bishop; he's a quick thinker and smooth talker and would twist things around like he's the victim. This man denied it all and didn't hold himself accountable. He decided to call a meeting at our home, which was very uncomfortable for me, with this young woman and the "Treasure" wife, only because she didn't want to involve her husband because her husband had already experienced some past church drama and hurt. Like previous experiences with the Bishop, he ended up taking over the conversation towards the end and started to cry at the table of the meeting like he was the victim. They both denied that nothing went on between them both, when I and the "Treasure's" wife knew deep within what took place between them both. I'm numb about this whole meeting but felt God's hand over me. God kept me humble, loving, merciful, and I didn't condemn her. God allowed me to speak with Grace in understanding that she was a baby in Christ and she had some deep issues that she needed help with. I blamed my husband the Bishop because he knew better. I was so disappointed and embarrassed by the Man of God I Married.

After all was over, the young lady's husband was highly upset and didn't want his family to come back to the ministry. All was kept a hush from the members, the "Treasures" husband, and the rest of the leaders in the church. The church was beginning to gain new members. People were walking in the door, and we all were working together as a team making sure all was in place. My baby girl and I knew to make ourselves available in every area that we saw a need. There were times after we would leave church, and he would complain that he needs help. Now, I've learned just to listen to him and not say a word because, as soon as I would say anything, he would begin to fuss, which was not a good place to be in, being in a marriage and walking on egg shells. The Bishop took charge of every area involving the church, including the finances, by choice. He never took the initiative to place any of us over the areas; he wanted full control but would complain to me and blame us as being unhelpful leaders.

The Bishop was not aware of his consistent outburst, abusive behavior and how much damage he was doing to me. He was draining me spiritually. All I've ever knew how to do during the hardest times of my life was run to Jesus, not say a word and sob on His lap. It's a lonely place when a wife can't express her heart to her husband about what he has done to hurt her, so she can properly heal. Late one night, we both were in the bed asleep and I heard somebody speaking in a strange tongue, so I woke up but didn't move. I noticed it was Bishop; the tongues continued. It sounded demonic, then I heard the Bishop say out loud "I Will Not Deny Christ." Now, I knew at the moment what was going on, so I didn't move, but I'm praying in my spirit. He woke up out of his dreams sweating, saying my God they were trying to make me deny Christ. I still didn't say a word. I knew deep down in my spirit that something was going to take place with him in the natural real soon. I got up out the bed and went downstairs and began to war on my husband's behalf.

It's something when a woman is in a unhealthy relationship; she doesn't recognize the issues at first, but as time goes on things begin to unfold. I was told by the wise long ago that you really don't know a person until you experience living behind closed doors with them. So much about this man begin to come to the surface that I didn't dig for. We were always to ourselves, spending a lot of time together, building ministry, vacationing and enjoying our new home, watching movies and playing around. It wasn't all bad experiences through the marriage, but there were a lot of hidden past secrets and unhealthy behaviors, outbursts, that I didn't know in the beginning about him that was unfolding as the years went on.

The Bishop was invited to a preaching engagement in Nicaragua, and we both were going to go, but I decided to stay home because my daughter was just starting school again, and the summer was just about over. We both discussed it all, and I knew that a team fast needed to be done to cover him as he travels to such a place. Well, we decided to fast together, but the fast was not united. Walking in this marriage with a saved man, my excitement of it and vision was totally different. I knew war was an assignment too, but I thought it would be like we both fasting and praying together, but no, that wasn't the case as time went on. He pulled further apart from the power of two in agreement. My spirit began to grieve because I knew we both needed to pray together, but Bishop still continued to do his own thing like it always had been. The Lord started to speak to me concerning all matters dealing with the Bishop, and those words were, "Share your heart with me, and I will handle him, and you remain loving and kind."

It was time for him to leave to go to Nicaragua for a week, and he's all ready to go. This dream that he had weeks before the trip was still in my spirit heavy, so I'm still at war against it in prayer. The church is being taken care of by me and a few of the leaders that remained attending the ministry. I had to minister to the people that coming Sunday, but my spirit just wouldn't rest about this trip and the Bishop. In my experiences concerning the Bishop, he could get a powerful prayer out when he was in the front of people but when he was away from church he didn't use that same power to protect us. He was really lacking within that area of prayer at home and in the marriage. I was always the one suggesting praying and scared to suggest that we fast together because of past experiences with him. His attitude and thinking he knew everything caused him to lack a strong discerning with people over the years I've been with him. He trusted everybody and would always say everybody is good people when he got what he wanted out of them. A person had to be in agreement with him, then he'd be well pleased with the soon to be relationship. About that time, he was in Nicaragua, and he would call me to share with me everything. Before he left, he was excited about the trip because him and the Pastor had discussed the amount of money he could receive from this trip. As I start to receive calls from him, he was up and down. One minute in his complaining mode, the next rejoicing; I was already familiar with my husband's split personality in our marriage. He also expressed to me that the few days he had been there, the Pastor that invited him had him preaching way too much, and they didn't agree upon that. One night, I was waiting on his call and didn't receive his call, and it wasn't the norm. Now, I'm like really concerned, and I decide to pray and afterward I went on Facebook and saw that he was on Facebook. I was shocked, because I've been waiting on his call all night. My intuition tells me to log into his Facebook account, and I see many inappropriate conversations with women in the past but a recent conversation with one of the women from where he was. This was the pastor's niece that invited him. I just couldn't believe what I was seeing at a time. When he called me, I asked why he didn't call me first, and he lied and said he just got out, and I mentioned I saw him logged on Facebook first before he called me, and he went off on me. Something that he always does when he's busted / wrong. Now I'm upset and decided that I'm not going to stand for his verbal abuse anymore, so I just hung up the phone, hoped he would calm down, and call back to apologize. He called back fussing and manipulating the conversation about the wrong he had done. I completely stopped answering the phone that night, cried, and went in prayer. The next day, later on that evening, he calls me like nothing happened, but the atmosphere on the phone was really strange. I know as a woman, a man knows the wrong he does; you don't have to keep harboring it over him. I cried and prayed the night before and turned him over to the Lord. At this point, I'm feeling as if I've let this man get away with so much that me and my feelings don't matter to him.

After his trip to Nicaragua was over, he came home a whole different person, like something was on him. He came back bragging about how they treated him better there than here. How he was able to talk to a Pastor that was in government and also what they discussed about him coming in partnership, making a whole lot of money together. He said this Pastor didn't want him talking to the other Pastors that he was with about this. I just listened because my spirit wasn't in agreement with these plans. I felt like something wasn't right with this Pastor he had been talking to, but I didn't say a word. I just listened and prayed in my spirit. The Bishop loved money, always talked about money and had a pattern of getting close to the wrong people just for what they had or what he could benefit from.

He never had the patience to wait his turn; he wanted everything quick, quick, quick. It's crazy because I remember every person that ever came in our lives that he told me about promised him things even before the marriage, and he held on to those people real tight and nothing ever manifested. When he returned, his behavior got worse. He was preaching in the pulpit saying things he shouldn't say, abusing the people of God, saying he had to take a trip back there because the people treated him better than his own church. He started threatening me by saying he's going to leave if I don't get right. His whole pattern at home changed. He's on the computer late at night until in the morning. He's also talking every day to somebody on the side, young women and all. The Bishop loved all of the attention. He was such an attention seeking man, and I've grown to see this over the years. One night I decided to run to the store ,and I left a tape recorder in the room where his office was hoping I was wrong about the change in him. I was out its been about 15 minutes and on my way back home he calls me asking me where I was and if I could go get him some ice cream. Normally when I'm out he's always calling saying can't wait till I get back home. My spirit was really uncomfortable about this call, but I knew I had a tape recorder on in his office already, but I was still praying the Lord let me be wrong about my husband. I got back home and brought the tape recorder in the room and put it in my ear plugs. In the beginning, I didn't hear anything and was rejoicing in my spirit because I was wrong. Just when I was about to cut the recorder off, I heard him talking to a young woman in Nicaragua. They were having a secret conversation. He was bragging, telling her his plans about how he was planning on leaving me. He was also lying to her, saying he was paying all the bills by himself. He told her that she needed to move from where she lived, and he would send her money to help her move. I listened to all of this trying to hold myself up because my daughter was in the house with us. I also knew how he would respond to this. I went in the room where he was and told him we needed to go to the church because it's an emergency, and I couldn't talk around my daughter. Bishop had been so disrespectful around my daughter many of the times and never felt remorseful about it before. We got to the church, and I hoped he would respect the house of the Lord. I sat on the alter and asked him why? I played the recording, and he just looked and got arrogant about it and said our marriage just didn't get this way; he blamed me by saying horrible things to me. This man wasn't the man I married; his eyes were so evil and his heart towards me was empty. He went on to say he didn't want the marriage, house, and the church anymore. I really couldn't believe what was really taking place before my eyes. I left him in the church by himself and drove home and sobbed the whole way there. I didn't know how in the world I made it home that night. Nothing, but God's Grace. I felt as if the life was taken out of me. I gave this man my heart and trusted him with it. Five years had passed in our marriage and we had served this man faithfully. We always brought him home surprise gifts when we would go out shopping. My baby girl never ever disrespected him; anything he asked her to do, she would do it. She loved him, she baked cakes for him, and she knew he loved her cakes. We both treated this man like a King behind closed doors. I aimed to please God in the marriage, my actions as a wife were consistent. This man really had it all, gifts given to him from heaven but became full of greed and very ungrateful. Something really took place in Nicaragua that only Him and God know about. What I saw in the spirit were witches.

    We both took a trip to Atlanta because he had a ministry engagement. As a wife, I always love supporting him in all his success. Serving in whatever area he needed me to serve in. On the ride to Atlanta, there was so much tension in the car that I could feel his mood. The drive there was so uncomfortable. I was praying in my spirit for peace on this trip. When we both made it to the hotel, all was well. At his speaking engagement, I was feeling such a detachment in his spirit when we got there, it was like he was there by himself. He didn't introduce me to anybody, even when he got up to speak, it was all about him. We both got back to the hotel room and were both lying in bed. He was talking on the phone to the Pastor in Nicaragua, making arrangements for himself to take a trip out there for the second time. Once he got off the phone, I asked him were we both taking the Nicaragua trip together because of the previous incident and he goes completely off by raising his voice saying, "No

I'm going on this trip by myself, and you are staying." I told him there was no reason for me to stay behind because we had leaders that could run the church. He was over the top disrespectful. By this time, it was time for us to check out, I got dressed, and we went down stairs with our suitcases; he got in the car and I was in the ladies' room crying, trying to get myself together to ride with him back home. When I got to the car, he was asking me what took me so long, and I told him I was in the bathroom. He goes completely off again and started driving fast down the high way speeding at 100 MPH, screaming saying, "I'm about to kill us today." Yelling this is driving me crazy. My heart drops in my stomach. I feel death at this moment. We are almost crossing through a 4-way intersection. I yell out, "NO,

NO, NO, I'm sorry!" Then he snaps back and slows down. Now we both are quiet in the car, and he drove to a gas station to get gas like nothing just happened. I got out of the car and called one of his best friends and told him what just happened. I refused to get back in the car with him. He did not apologize, he just stared a mean and evil look saying, "No you just get in the car." His friend was now convinced that my husband had a serious problem. In my mind, I was thinking, "My God, what have I Married?" This man almost killed the both of us.

I invited a client to the ministry. During this time, my client was writing checks to the church and sending them to a Post Office Box in the Bishop's name. The church's finance team was totally unaware of this. Bishop had finally put a finance team together after 4 years. The "Treasure Couple" was a part of the finance team and called a meeting because things were looking suspicious with the money. Bishop was a very defensive man, he had an attitude with them and wanted to know what the meeting was about, but they didn't want to go into details. During this time, I was quiet, and the bishop was talking continuously to his bishop friend on the phone very negatively concerning the "Treasures Couple". I was praying for peace during this time because I was not sure how the Bishop would respond in this meeting. The meeting started and the "Treasures Couple" pulled out folders with copies of the church bank statements on them. Bishop was very quiet and "Treasures Couple" was very upset. They questioned my husband about why checks were being written out to the church, and the money was being taken out of the church account? He became defensive all the more and him and the "Treasures Wife" started to argue. I really couldn't believe what was taking place in the Lord's house. So, I tried to calm my husband down and then the "Treasures husband" jumped up. So, the "Treasure wife" and I walk out of the room and we left the men to talk. After they talked, and my husband cried, we both made an agreement to pay the money back to the church. When we left the church, we were both quiet. I was praying in the spirit to pray against him attacking me. He asked me what I thought, and I responded, "why didn't you tell me this before we went into this meeting, that my client was sending checks to your post office box and you were cashing them out?" He looked at me and started "going off" on me, he said that my client told him that the checks were for him and that we could call him if I wanted to. I said, "yes, let's call him." At this point, I didn't know what to believe from the man I married anymore. He had so many secrets from the very beginning and now truth was starting to reveal itself. I tried not to hold him hostage for his past because I really didn't care about his past but only our future together.

The entire night he was manipulating and blaming me. Saying I didn't take up for him, and so on. He also was on the phone with his friends telling them I was wrong and that he was about to remove the "Treasures Couple" off the church bank account. He didn't realize that the enemy was using him to attack these people and retaliate. My heart was so broken. I just dropped down on the bathroom floor sobbing, asking the Lord to forgive us both as His leaders and to give me the strength to handle this as his wife. This was the silent cry of a First Lady. I was hurting, but he was always concerned about himself and never others. The next morning, he woke up angry and we both went to the bank to remove the "Treasures Couple" off the church bank account. They found out and they decided to leave the church, it was what the bishop wanted.

    I knew this was not the end of the verbal abuse, I had to deal with this behind closed doors. I was his main target now. I was verbally abused everyday by him. He would blame me and talk about me negatively to other people. My feelings, nor voice did not matter. I sat in silence and prayed that the Lord would keep me and heal my husband. The Bishop had bitterness towards everything and everybody. He didn't care about our church family. He was planning to close the church down and walk out of the marriage as well. His secrets were being exposed. Every day he would come and talk to me to manipulate me by telling me he was tired, and he's been unhappy for years in the marriage. He was trying to turn all tables on me. Time and truth was revealing itself. His Leadership behavior was unacceptable from the very beginning.

Chapter 7

Just when I thought things could not get any worse. My mom was rushed to the hospital for extreme dehydration. My mom had previously beaten stage 4 ovarian cancer 2 years prior, and it returned and travelled to her lungs, leaving her in a fight for her life. This was a trying time for me, with all that was going on with Bishop, the church, and my marriage. I was faced with the truth that my mom was sick, and her health was deteriorating daily. However, this did not move the Bishop. He kept doing what he was doing and was not even concerned the least bit about my mom. Once again, he was only concerned about himself. We, by this time, had started to sleep in separate rooms. My husband, the Bishop was sleeping in the guest bedroom. He would wear his wedding band off and on. When I came home from seeing my mom at the hospital, he was not concerned about her; he started to question me and taunt me by saying that the marriage was over and that he no longer wanted to be with me. I was torn because this was not something I wanted to hear while my mom was sick. He was very restless at this point in the marriage; he would pace the floor at night, and it was extremely uncomfortable for me. He would be on social media all day and was sexually aggressive in the marriage towards me, often times pulling out the bible and manipulating me to have sex. This was extremely heart wrenching because I knew he did not treat me like a wife. By this time, the bishop was planning to move 30 minutes from our house and was really trying to punish me and retaliate.

Through all of this, I was still doing what the bible wanted me to do as a wife. I would still cook, clean, and manage the household, I would even still have sex. This was me doing what was right out of my love for the Lord. Bishop was very watchful over me, but not in a good way. It was as if this spirit was watching me to see how it could tear me down. This placed a burden on me to be careful what I said around him. I remained silent during this time with minimal conversation. Bishop was writing a book at this time and, come to find out, this was not his first book; he would write books to try to cover up his mistakes from the past in order to change and paint how people see him. Supposedly, I was the evil one in this story, just as were all the other women.

It seemed like I would struggle with him forever. I was at a point to where being in my own home was not peaceful nor satisfying. During the day, I would wait for the bus to pick my daughter up for 6AM, go to a hotel and go back home at 3PM. I did not want my daughter to see me in that condition. I was so broken, but through my brokenness, I would fight on to pray and fast. I went to the hotel as a way of being in my prayer closet. The Lord was very firm with me about not letting the Bishop see me broken down and confused. I did not want to encourage his shenanigans any longer, so this was my way to vent and cry out to the Lord for help. I was very careful when the Holy

Spirit revealed things to me. I was cautious about what I shared with him and what emotions I displayed when I was around him. He was not aware that I had the code to his voicemail and his brief case. I knew of all his future plans, and I was able to hear from the women he was talking to. He was not aware that I had that or knew of his plans. During this time however, the Lord did not release me to say anything; I was still quiet and remained the same. As he was planning to move away, I find out that he was planning to shut down the church and ministry. He was not showing up for bible study, people were calling and asking about what was going on. He didn't care about anyone. He closed the church down and walked out of the marriage as well because his secrets were exposed. Every day he would try to manipulate me. He was trying to turn all tables on me. I had to stop listening to the ministry radio station because he was attacking me through his interviews with people. He was having conversations with so many different women, and also the young lady in Nicaragua.

By this time, my body was drained, my heart was heavy, and I was feeling so alone, The Holy Spirit unctioned me to start fasting and to get with my best friend and start praying for my husband. So, we began praying for my husband nonstop. It went on for three months. By that time, there were so many forces over my husband that were controlling him to attack me every day. From the beginning of our marriage, we were very close, our routine weekly was to run our business errands together. It was to the point where he had expressed his anger towards me another way, by the music he would play when I would ride with him anywhere. He would play oldie but goodies music like "Love and happiness" and many other songs he saved through his music playlist the night before. It was like he was out to destroy me. I was silent while walking through this process, crying / bleeding on the inside. I watched the evil forces of personalities use him daily.

My mom passed away during this time, and even though my mother was gone, I knew I had to push through. I was still running my business in the perfection I was charged to do by God, answering the business phone like nothing happened. Life still went on. The bishop found out that my mom passed away from my brother and questioned me about why I didn't call to tell him about mom passing away. I just could not open up to him, nor would I trust him enough to open up to him. When he confronted me about it, I was quiet and said nothing. After all his wondering, he still did not show up to the funeral, even though he always said that he was closer to my mom than his own mom. He chose to go on the trip Nicaragua during that time.

    I still could not show the bishop that I was bleeding on the inside. People would see him and didn't like what was going on with him and I. The Bishop was very prideful at this time and had so much going on that no one could correct him. By this time, I was still not responding to him. I would often recall what my mom would tell me, "If something is not right, don't stay in it." I joined a prayer group at a predominantly white church with elderly white women that had been praying for over 20 years every day. I even took classes there and was extremely grateful to have taken a believer's authority class. I was happy to be in a place where no one knew me, and I was receiving spiritual uplifting. During this time, Bishop got a lawyer, and I was going to court for the divorce. I was not directed by the Holy Spirit at that time to get a lawyer, so I just let things play out.

Bishop was coming back and forth from the house, bullying me, and saying horrible things to me in front of my daughter. He had his lawyers calling me and trying to get me to sign papers to agree with what he wanted me to do. Bishop was used to getting his way. During this time, he would come to the house with a realtor. I had so much fear and anxiety surrounding this relationship, these were issues I developed as a result of the abuse. This was my grieving stage. There were times when I would wake up and the Holy Spirit would tell me to leave the house. God was clothing me because I did not have any more strength. Through all of this, my heart is still pure towards my husband and all of my prayer partners are in agreement with me for the soul of my marriage and my husband's return back home in his right mind. With all of the aggressive ongoing court dates, nothing happened. It was like God had my daughter and I safe in a bubble so all that the sprit that was controlling him to do to us didn't work. Finally, we had a court date that was set for next year, so my Daughter and I went on a trip to Dominica on a cruise. It was a time of refreshing for us. Bishop came to the house the day we got back; he wanted to talk to me. I guess I was so far removed from him, and he was not getting a response from me, which bothered him. He asked me to sit down and talk and asked if I would sale the house. Of course I am completely compliant and not fighting back. I am still quiet and not aggressively opposing. After he left the house, he called me 20 minutes later asking did I still love him, and I paused for a minute and I told him yes, and he told me he was sorry. At this time, I felt like this was an answered prayer because I was praying for him for so long. SO, he moved back home and said that he would put building the marriage first and nothing before the marriage. However, his actions were contradictory and nothing he promised. I told him I was not the same woman and that things were equal, and I would no longer be silent. When he apologized, I took him back in, and we attempted to solve things and work things out. I intuitively knew later on after taking him back that it was about money. One day, the Holy Spirit told me to take some of my money out of the account and transfer it into another account. I was obedient. During this time, I also had a dream about a python. Immediately, the Holy Spirit spoke to me and said, "He has come back to suck the life out of you." The next morning, it was like I was dealing with the old person again, Bishop called me in his office and spoke to me as if I was a child, demanding that I show him my bank account balances. This revealed his true colors. He would use me to pay all of his bills and wipe out the accounts. He also agreed to go to counseling the second time around; however, that did not work out because of pride. I picked a really meek pastor at a local church to try to sort out our issues in marriage. When I was in counseling and said how I felt, he would get mad and felt embarrassed and would tell the pastor this is not working; he didn't want to be married anymore. After I left out of the session, he handed him a book that he wrote. Bishop hated to be wrong, he was not used to people seeing his true colors even though people always did.

After all of this, he attempted to get me to sign papers without reading through the documents. He wanted a divorce again. I had taken my daughter through this once and I didn't feel right doing this again. The divorce case had to start all over again and boy was he mad. He left a 2nd time. The first time he left, I didn't show him my brokenness, but the 2nd time, I decide to speak and share my heart with him and asked him what is going on. Why is he doing this to us again? He looked at me with a evil look in his eyes and said, "I am not leaving in front of Bri, I will wait until she gets on the bus for school in the morning." While, in the beginning, he promised my daughter he would be a father, he was not concerned about her at all in the end. By this time, the Lord released me to get a lawyer. I did it! I was not upset because if I would have gotten an attorney earlier, I would have lost money. This time I was going in all the way. The lawyer investigated many things and come to find out, Bishop was making close to 10k a month when everything was disclosed to me. He was transferring a lot of money; we also saw that he opened a Jeweler's account and that this was evidence of what he was planning to do, marry other women, which was told to me in the beginning by others. It was difficult for me to handle all of this, but in the end, the divorce went through, and I was freed from the torments of oppression. Through all of this, the truth hurts, but the truth revealed itself and made me free.

Chapter 8

Through the Eyes of Bri

Growing up, I witnessed my mother being an independent hardworking single mother to 3 kids. My mom always made sure we were good and had everything we "needed," and she never once complained about it. People used to tell my mom, when I was a baby, that I would be her angel and always cover her.

My dad was incarcerated since I was born, so I really didn't grow up with that father figure in my life. We would always go see him where he was incarcerated, but I was so young I really didn't understand nothing that was going on. Some of the times, when we went to see him, I would cry the whole time. By the age of 7, my dad was released and was able to come home. I was happy when he first arrived because what girl wouldn't be happy to see their daddy after a long time. My mama helped my daddy start his life fresh, bought him all new things, and helped him get back on his feet by finding a job. She had seen potential in him and knew that he was a changed man. My dad tried to build a relationship with me and my brother, but it was more like buying our love. When my mom and him had gotten a divorce, everything changed; he started to be the old him. I used to see my daddy every day, then it was like every 3 weeks or every other month when he wanted to show up. Our relationship was not like the typical daddy daughter relationship; it was like a friendship. He didn't care what we called him or how we talked to him. On my birthdays, he would come get me and take me to get whatever I wanted and bring me back home. I am not gone lie, my daddy always made sure we were good and got what we wanted. Three years after the divorce, my mom came into my room and said, "Bri your daddy died." It hit me, and I cried because I just started to get to know my dad and build a better relationship with him, and he left so soon. My stepdad to be had volunteered to preach at the funeral. I didn't go up the alter to see him because I didn't want to see my dad like that. Even though I didn't get to build the relationship I wanted with him, I loved him with all my heart. My mom was the strongest out of us all; she continued to make sure my dad was laid to rest the right way and her kids were straight through it all. Though they couldn't work things out, she continued to love him like a mature person would do.

    My mom continued on her life and started to become closer to the Bishop. He seemed to be "all about" my mom when I first met him. He was funny and very nice; he was trying to do anything for us to like him and become comfortable with him and accept him. Me being me, I only wanted my mama to be with my daddy and not be with anybody else. But, hey. I couldn't be selfish. Who doesn't want their mother to be happy? My mom and bishop finally got married, and it was a beautiful experience to be the flower girl. That day was so stressful; my mom was late for her own wedding (lol) due to traffic. My mom looked so happy that night, it was amazing! All of our family and friends were there congratulating her and praying my mom and Bishop see many years together.

Less than a year later, we finally were moving from our old house to the house we always dreamed about! I was kind of skeptical about moving from Kenner (a busy city) to Ponchatoula (country/ quiet city), but the house was priceless. 4 bed rooms and 2 1/2 bathrooms, upstairs and downstairs, it was everything I imagined. When we first toured the house, I ran upstairs and went in a room farthest to the back and said, "This is my room." and everybody laughed. Starting school, entering 5th grade was very scary; I didn't know anybody, plus I was shy. I was thinking to myself, this school is way easier than Kenner schools. It was a breeze! I loved everything about Ponchatoula and really enjoyed living out here.

Growing up around the age of 10-16, Bishop was like a father to me; he helped me with my school work and gave me wise tutoring with life goals and how I should stay focused and make good grades. Sometimes I used to be like he's aggravating and he gets on my nerves, but I couldn't do anything about it. It took my Grandma a long time to start liking him; she doesn't just become cool with anybody, she sits back and watch lol. Before my grandma died she did say, when she first meets Bishop, there was something about him that she couldn't put her hand on at that moment. During the time Bishop lived with us, him and my mother would always get into it about crazy things; he would like to argue about everything! I know a child would always take up for their mom, but I could see that she was "right" every time. When me and my mom would go shop, we would have to hide bags in the trunk because he would want to fuss about her buying stuff. That's really crazy though; sometimes I would feel a dislike for him because of the way he acts and argues about everything. He would even want to argue and have attitudes in front of my family, and that's what made my family dislike him. Things started to shift to an end; my mom and Bishop were outgrowing each other. My mom was the best thing that could ever happen in his life. Without my mom loving on him, supporting and tolerating his mixed moods, he wouldn't have had what he left with. I won't sugar coat anything; my mama is a real one. She sticks in there until the end when there's nothing more to fight for. In July 2016, he left us, moved out, and abandoned us. It was something over him that made him do it or even think of doing it. My mom was so heartbroken, it was so sad; I would never want to see my mom in that emotional state again. My grandma died in July, and he didn't even attend the funeral or ask my mom was she okay What kind of man would do that? A couple months later he apologized to my mom and moved back in; it was all fine, but after 3 weeks, it happened again. He moved out for the second time, so you know what that meant. I'm thinking mental issues – he's a confused man. My mom was trying to fight for the marriage as hard as she could, but she finally realized it isn't worth it! My mom used to always ask me how I felt about him leaving and am I hurting? To be honest, I really didn't care if he left because I felt he was using my mom and was taking her for granted. I began to dislike him; I peeped a lot of things about him that just didn't settle in me. During the time of us grieving over my grandmother's death, the Bishop forced courts dates to court dates and came over to the house angry, bullying my mom every other day; they finally gotten a divorce. My mom deserves better a man who is going to love her for who she is, an independent man, a man who's for God, a man who's a replica of her! Bishop didn't get the memo to do anything he vowed to her. He changed up and lucked out on the best thing that could ever happen to his future.

Through My Eyes

My mother is an Entrepreneur. She can be by herself and doesn't need the likes, dislikes of people to be who she is. She is her own Boss and provider by the Grace of God. I witnessed so many miracles in my life and my mom's life. She always was there for me when I needed her the most. She is always there for people and will give her all up for anybody. She puts everyone before herself. It is now her time to shine and live the life she was made to live. She works hard for the things she has and is going to have in due time. Now when you read this, I want you to know "You can do all things through Christ who strengthens You." Let God be the head of your life; He, with all the answers, is who you need ... I use my mom for example because she's been through the most but still managed to be the best she can be. My mom now is in the process of pursuing many things on the horizon for us that I can't speak about. I was taught as a child don't tell mama business because wisdom is moving in silence. She worked hard for what she wants; don't judge a book by its cover. I love you so much mom. Thanks for being there for me; I'm always there when you need me.

Tracy's Words

We were all born with wings, but it's all about learning how to fly. There were times through this journey, while traveling, we experienced some of the bumps and bruises of life. These bumps and bruises would cause one to never trust or love again. However, there is Perfect Love that casts out all fear; it came directly from God, who enabled us to fly again. This type of love keeps us from falling and allows us to fly high above the ground!

"Never Be Afraid to Fly Again " regardless of what God allowed you to experience. He knew from the beginning, you were well qualified for it, and there were other people in mind that you will be helping along the way. It's never about you, it's all about God, getting His Glory out of your story!

I asked the Lord, "How did I get entangled in something like this when I held myself and prayed and asked you for the right husband?" I was cautious and waited on the Lord. God spoke to me and said, "This is your cross that I trust you with, and there are other Women and Men in mind that I trust you to tell your story to, and all your living is for my Glory. I gave you life, not bishop."

Writing this book has truly taken me out of my comfort zone. It's been much warfare, deliverance, and also very emotional for me at the same time. But I'm very humble to have been able to get this assignment done through all the chaos that was around me. Thank God for His protection of a soundproof realm that kept me focused and able to talk about my story for the last time.

www.ingramcontent.com/pod-product-compliance
Lightning Source LLC
Chambersburg PA
CBHW032125090426
42743CB00007B/467